The Blooming Poet

Rose Haslbauer

BookLeaf Publishing

India | USA | UK

Presentation by *BookLeaf Publishing*

Web: www.bookleafpub.com

E-mail: info@bookleafpub.com

ISBN: 9789360946845

First edition 2024

Candid Canvas (2016)

Life is like art,
full of intricate swirls and lines.
You are the sculptor,
the paintbrush, the pencil,
but one without an eraser.
There's no undo button, no reverse
because life is not meant to be rehearsed
or practiced until it reaches your
personal standard of perfection.
It's meant to be a reflection
of where you currently are.

Life is meant to be messy,
with paint splattered and points scattered
into a design that seems incomprehensible,
unnecessary and disposable.
But as it goes, beauty is in the eye of the
beholder
and as you grow wiser and older,
the less you magnify into your work.
You don't analyze each regret, mistake and error,
begin to step back and find that
the further you go, the more it comes together.

And that garbled mess you used to see?
It has transformed right before your eyes
to become a masterpiece: you.

Fairest (2016)

Magic mirror on the wall,
who's the fairest of them all?
I know it's not you
and for sure it's not me
for we are so filled with the
vice that clouds our sanity and
makes an animal out of me.
We feel the depravity
when the number of likes
doesn't reach the mass capacity
of our laughably sensitive egos.
We rely on sensuality and
perverted sexuality all too often
and all too craftily.
It's become a commonality
that muddles our mentality,
eating away at us like a cavity.
It finds hospitality within
the crevices of humanity,
found within the physicality
of our very anatomy.
It makes a pageantry
of our very existence.
I'm so sick of the barbarity
of this abnormal normality
of modern society, vanity.

Icarus (2018)

They say to reach for the moon because then
you'll land among stars.
Well, if that's the case, then I will be aiming for
the sun.
I've run out of ground to run upon and sky to
sail.
I don't care if my hopes derail - that's what
they're made for, right?
To carry you as you take flight towards wherever
you're meant to go
or whoever you're meant to be - or maybe that's
just me.

You see, too many people get comfortable with
where they are
but we were not made for that, we were made
for greatness.
Unfortunately, that route isn't painless because
of the process
of being and becoming who you're meant to be
requires
blood, sweat, tears, and a whole lot of your
heart.
Maybe you'd rather not go through that and just
settle.

And that's fine, since you will find yourself
sitting among the stars.
Stars are beautiful, but plentiful, diminishing
their worth
and making them as common as the air we
breathe on earth.

So why not shoot for the sun instead, for if your
wings being to melt
from flying too closely, you'll still land safely on
the rocky ground
of the moon instead, as if you had already had it
all planned.

Chill

Chilled, just like the moment the air hits you as
you leave your cocoon bed.
Chilled, just like the frosted dew displayed on
the windshield of your car.
Chilled, just like the winter air that makes your
cheeks flushed and rosy.
Chill, just like you try to remain as you sit
through rush hour traffic.
Chilled, just like the moment the cold seeps in as
you leave your car.
Chill, just like you try to act to stand out and
remain unnoticed all at once.
Chill, just like you try to portray yourself to be
through the lens of social media.
Chill, just like we try to act be to avoid scrutiny
that comes with being individual.
Chill, just like our words, quick to label, judge
and speak ill of other people.
Chilled, just like our minds, frozen by the lack
of introspective thought.
Chilled, just like our hardened hearts, trained to
shield ourselves and lash out.
Chilled, just like our scars and mental to keep
our brokenness unseen.
Chill, just like we really truly ought not to be.

Small Joys

We often look for light and joy in the grandiose,
the things that are unmistakable in their glory
when really, the greatest things in our lives
are in the everyday moments we overlook.

There's a joy to be found in belly laughter
that erupts, wanes, and erupts once again
from a joke that was not even that funny,
but one's laughter is too contagious to stop.

There's a joy to be found in what is fresh,
from driving down a newly paved road
after it had been riddled with potholes,
or a still-warm batch of cookies that
you find sticking to the roof of your mouth.

There is a joy to be found in nature too, from
soaking in the last lights and colors of a sunset
or watching it peek over the horizon at dawn,
that reminds you that each day is a blessing.

There is a joy to be found on the rainy days too,
with the smell of the rain wafting in your nose
when you finally step outside to brave the storm

or the coziness of a warm blanket draped over
you
protecting you from the elements raging outside.

There's a joy to be found in small
accomplishments
like finding and placing the final piece of a
puzzle,
or the finality of closing a book that you had
read,
or the first sip of a cold drink or climbing into
bed
after having put in a full day's effort of hard
work.

There's a joy to be found in relationships we
keep,
from the feeling of fingers interlocking with
yours,
genuinely listening to your answer of "how are
you,"
or that moment of eye contact and sly smile
that pairs with inside jokes only you and the
other know.

When we really come to stop and think about it
all,
the grandiose things in life are just singular
moments.

It is the little things that add up repeatedly each
day,
adding up to a sum of joy that is infinitely
beautiful.

Pottery (2016)

I'm like a piece of pottery, but one that is old and
cracked.
It's been knocked down and broken, but
somehow remains intact
because after all the pieces fall, I pick them up
part by part,
pasting them together again to form a new piece
of art.

Unfortunately it's not as pretty as it once used to
be
but it's the very best I could do since there's only
one of me.
On a ledge once again it sits, but when I see it
collecting dust,
I manage to find trouble that makes it all
combust.

Something will stir its stand and I'll watch it
sway side to side
until it settles down so I can knock it myself
with power amplified.
I don't mean to do it, since I never want it to
truly break,

but for some reason, a mess is all that I can seem
to make.

It causes me to fall apart and reopen all of my
old wounds,
so I get down on my knees to pick up all the
remaining ruins.
Piece by piece I collect, while grabbing the tape
and glue,
so that I can, once again, create and break
myself anew.

Outside (2021)

I feel like I'm viewing the world
and life happening around me
through a window glass -
close enough to see everything
but too far away to be present.
I feel like I'm on the outside of myself.
I long to reach through the glass
and be inside with everyone else,
but the windowpane is nailed shut.
How do I open the window now
without cutting myself on the glass?

Spoiled

After a long night of tears and rainfall,
the sun and my hope begin to rise.
The day blooms slowly and carefully
with its bud facing the warm beams.
Petals unravel and stretch open
With the possibility of feeling joy.

I am the gardener whose job is to
nourish the plant with water and love.
But instead sometimes begin to pour
and cannot stop the tip of the hand.
The bud's stem is fragile and folds
all while the roots begin to drown.

All in one moment and one movement,
all of the hope and glimmer of light
that came with the new day dawning
has faded back into the grey darkness.
Just like that, the feeling of hope and joy
has been spoilt and left to rot in the sun.

Little Monsters

As a kid, I believed the nighttime monsters
resided under my bed,
but as I grew older, I realized that they exist at
night in my head.
The darkness creeps in and releases all of my
anxieties and fears,
quietly tormenting my mind until dawn, when
the sun reappears.

I can normally control my emotions and keep
the monsters at bay,
put on a nice smile, a brave face, and make it
through each day.
But as the sun sets, so does my strength to fight
the inner beasts,
and once the moon fully rises, the monsters will
begin their feast.

The monsters point out my insecurities, deepest
wounds, and flaws,
managing their way under my thick skin with
sharp teeth and claws.
Relying on my willpower and prayer to fight
them off, I earnestly try,

but it seems most nights these days, the beasts
berate me until I cry.

Leaving me beaten and worn, the monsters
finally allow me to rest,
and once the sun returns, there is no sign of this
unwelcome guest.
But the truth is that they're just dormant in the
shadows of my mind,
because once evening comes around again,
they're never far behind.

Stay (2010)

I want to fix humanity.
I can't - welcome to reality.
There's so much I miss,
those moments of pure bliss.
There's so much I want to tell
but am unheard even when I yell.

People hold onto broken hearts
while it seems hope is falling apart.
We fight with friends and family
but can't we just live happily?

There's burdens when we're awake
so we go through the motions to make
it seem like everything is fine
and keep trying to pass the time.
But we stumble down and cry
Or stay up wishing on stars late at night.

We keep counting our sheep
But still can't manage to get sleep.
We need some help from above
To help us face what we're scared.

Everyday I pray,

I ask for everything to turn out okay.
Praying day by day,
Please listen to what I have to say.
Burst into tears, I may,
God, if you're there, say hey.
Don't push me away,
Take a seat and stay.

Praise (2013)

Praise to Sundays in autumn,
as we watch the Giants game.
Linemen become soldiers,
with stiff arms their shields,
as they tackle their way through.

Praise to my dad shouting
at the sight of an interception.
But he changes his tune
when the word touchdown rings out
and Tiki celebrates in the end zone.

Praise to the halftime reports
that no one seems to listen to.
It's then that we bundle up
ready to fight the approaching winter
and the frosty chill that comes with it.

Praise to my brothers
who tackle me as I catch the ball
thrown gently by my dad.
I fall into the fresh, crisp leaves
and presume it was just an accident.

Praise to our muddy shoes

almost as worn out as we are
when we trudge back inside,
undoubtedly annoying my mom
who had just cleaned the floors.

Praise to my parents who cook.
It's most likely sparkly chicken,
the family staple meal we love,
presented on the wooden table
standing proudly at the heart of the kitchen.

Praise to my brother Dan.
The room becomes his stage
as he acts out the highlights of the day
and makes it overly dramatic
for our own entertainment.

Praise to his twin Eric.
His laughter is contagious,
always making you laugh along
and makes you tear up
from laughing too hard.

Praise to dessert.
Dan and Dad choose salty,
Eric and mom sweet,
and me with a bowl of ice cream,
but only if drowned in chocolate syrup.

Praise to playing "run away" after.
Lights off, bellies full and spirits high,
we run and scream until we're caught
or until we cramp up from running around
and need to pause to cuddle up instead.

Praise to my old bedtime.
I hated it because I was "never tired,"
and I'd often sneak out of my bed,
but I loved it because it meant getting
a goodnight hug and kiss from the ones I love
most.

So praise Sunday football games.
Praise sweet memories.
Praise sparkly chicken.
Praise belly laughs.
Praise bedtime.
Praise family.
Praise mud.
Praise.

Proverbs 31:25 (2017)

Sometimes I feel like a paradox to this quote
because I try to be clothed with strength,
but if someone were to read the poems I write,
they would see how weak I truly am inside
and be aware of the fragility of my very soul.
My icy shield is my masked smile that
hides a beaten down, burnt out, and tired girl.

With the point of dignity, I'm caught between
having too little of it and holding far too much.
I know to never settle, but sometimes aim too
high
and follow my heart instead of following my
mind.

Then there's the part about the future as well.
I try not to act like I don't think about it much,
but in truth, I find I exist in the past and yet
always seem to be wish to be in what lies ahead.
I don't know where I am going or even where I
am now.
So yes, you may see me laughing, but it is in
spite
rather than because my heart is without fear.

Lamentations and Revelations

My Lament:
We're told to offer things up to God,
but the things I hold feel insulting.
Why give Him heartache and doubt
and my many waves of sadness?
They say that He will carry the load
and to look at the one set of footprints
when the burdens get too heavy,
but then why am I still being crushed?
I'm told to believe God loves and sees all,
which includes me and my heart,
but Lord, when will I receive respite
and when will I finally feel whole?
I believe that I am practically shouting,
saying that I need you here with me,
but all I hear is silence that makes me
question if you can even hear my amen.

God's Promise:
I say to you, turn your anxieties to me
and let me know of every tear that falls,
for they do not insult, but draw me closer.
For in your pain, you will find my grace.
I say to you, I cannot carry all you hold,

but I will walk with you in every step.
You may carry your many burdens, but
I am the guiding light for your path.
I say to you, when you bear your wounds,
I am found within that broken heart.
It may be difficult to dig into the pain,
but you will find me already there waiting.
I say to you, you are already whole
even when you feel most fractured.
Respite will come when you learn to rest
by finally and truly welcoming my embrace.
I say to you, whether you shout it or
whisper it quietly through your tears,
I can hear your amen that you believe.
And for that, no, I will never leave.

Heaven

They say we won't know what heaven is like
until the day we pass away and arrive
at the feet of St. Peter and the pearly gates.
We are told we can only understand heaven
through elaborate metaphors and stories,
full of complex language and comparisons
that help us to see what its beauty is really like
or how we can become worthy of a place there.
We are told it will be a mystery of death
but the truth is that I already know heaven,
what it is like and seen glimpses of it in my life.
In fact, I've even been to heaven myself.

For heaven is as simple as the colors of the
sunset
reflecting off the worlds' irises and rolling tides.
Heaven is hearing the pure and unadulterated joy
that comes with hearing a baby's belly laugh.
Heaven is the feeling of a smile on someone's
face
as you gently envelope them in a warm embrace.
Heaven is the welcoming aroma that hits your
nose
when you open the door when you arrive home.

Heaven is the gentle thump of a heartbeat you
hear
as you rest your head on someone's chest.
Heaven is the feeling of unconditional love you
receive
and fully knowing and believing you're worthy
of it.

Those People (2013)

You know those people you feel you've always
known
even though you only met them after you had
grown?
Those are some of the absolute best people.
They know you as the product or aftermath,
the outcome of whatever path life had led you
down.
Though they might not have seen you sprout
and watched you blossom from the ground up,
they know that you did.
They know it was most likely a bumpy ride,
and even if they weren't right next to your side,
they know that someone else was, most likely
the same thing that happened to them at some
point.
It's what makes them so enticing and kind of
people
you find yourself wanting to share things with
that let them know your story, your history,
where you came from,
where you fell,
where you've risen to,
and where you aspire to go next.
You never know, when you hear their story,
maybe they're traveling in the same direction as
you.

As If

I like the way our hands fit together
and the way they just seem to meld,
as if the world knew my hand would be held.
I like the way your arms wrap me tight
like a sturdy refuge away from distress,
as if the world knew it would be my safe
fortress.
I like the way that your name flows
easily off of my lips and tongue,
as if the world knew it would be my favorite
song.

But more than all of the physical things,
I really like the way you joke around
and can always make me laugh,
as if the world knew you'd be my comedic half.
I really like the way we have our differences
but always seem to be on the same page,
as if the world knew we would reach this stage.
I really like the way you're so respectful
always being so caring and sweet,
as if the world knew our hearts would meet.

But most importantly and most of all,
I love the way you make me feel

and bring so much happiness to my heart,
as if the world knew I'd see you're a work of art.
I love the way I can be myself with you
vulnerable, strong, weak and real,
as if the world knew the ways you'd help me
heal.
I love the way I feel so at home with you
a comfortable space that came with time,
as if the world knew I'd be yours and you'd be
mine.

Mosaic

I collect each piece of you bit by bit.
Some pieces are complete and whole,
easy to read, simple to understand,
and I can quickly see its place in
the puzzle of you and your soul.

Other pieces are smaller and scattered,
a little more complicated but still clear
so I can still identify where it's meant
to go within the mosaic image of you.

Others are even tinier with sharp edges,
hard to open up about and can sting
but are vital to understanding and
work as the glue to some other pieces.

Finally there are still many parts hidden,
undiscovered in the shadows of your soul,
waiting to be seen and loved all the same
completing the masterpiece of you, my love.

Scars

The scars you carry in your heart
are laid out for me like a map.
I am the new intrepid explorer
navigating without a compass.
but onward I must press because
on the days when I reach the top,
I am bathed in your bright sunlight.

Please let your words and stories
act as my directions and guide
so that I know where to safely go.
You need not to soften or censor
things with me for I won't be shaken
but rather cling to every word like
it is my lifeline to understanding.

Please let your faults and failures
be where I shine a light on how it
has made you an even better person.
You need not be ashamed or shy
about the downfalls for I won't judge
but rather kiss every invisible wound
like it is the glue to the collage of you.

Please let your hopes and your joys

be where I can put down my anchor
and slowly root and plant myself.
You need not ask or wonder about
if or how long I will rest in that place
but rather know that I plan to stay
like it is my home welcoming me in.

Please let me explore your kind heart
and see every aspect of who you are
because it is the real you that I love.
You need not care or be troubled
that the scars you carry may stay
for I will gently love each little mark
until it feels like they've faded away.

Slow Dance

Falling for you is like a first slow dance.
You move cautiously and nervously,
mindful to not step on any toes.
But when you're being held securely,
you can slowly find your feet
and begin to follow the other's lead
until you find yourself perfectly in line,
synchronizing your movements
in a way that makes the whole room
think you were meant to dance together.
And the beautiful thing is that you are.
It just was never the right moment
to ask your partner to take your hand
and begin the slow dance with you.
But now that you have begun,
you never want to leave the dance floor,
or at least not without your partner
and their steady hand holding yours.